P9-CND-382

Real Women Have Curves

A comedy by

JOSEFINA LÓPEZ

Dramatic Publishing Company
Woodstock, Illinois • Australia • New Zealand • South Africa

IMPORTANT BILLING AND CREDIT REQUIREMENTS

All producers of the play *must* give credit to the author of the play in all programs distributed in connection with performances of the play and in all instances in which the title of the play appears for purposes of advertising, publicizing or otherwise exploiting the play and/or a production. The name of the author *must* also appear on a separate line, on which no other name appears, immediately following the title, and *must* appear in size of type not less than fifty percent (50%) the size of the title type. Biographical information on the author, if included in the playbook, may be used in all programs. *In all programs this notice must appear:*

"Produced by special arrangement with
THE DRAMATIC PUBLISHING COMPANY, INC., of Woodstock, Illinois."

Real Women Have Curves
is dedicated to the women on whom these
characters are loosely based, my mother Catalina Perales
and my sister Esther López, S. Orbach, the author of
Fat Is a Feminist Issue, and to all the undocumented
and now documented garment workers of Los Angeles.

Real Women Have Curves was first presented by El Teatro De La Esperanza at the Mission Cultural Center in San Francisco, California, May 25, 1990. The production was directed by Hector Correa; set design by Kate Boyd; light design by Elaine Buckholtz; costume design by Anastasia Powers. The cast was as follows:

ANA .... Francine Torres
ESTELA .... Jennifer Proctor
CARMEN .... Marta Del Rio
PANCHA .... Tessa Koning-Martinez
ROSALI .... Miraida Ríos

ACKNOWLEDGMENTS

Special thanks to: God, Catalina and Rosendo López, Keisuke Fukuda, Bill Virchis, Lupe Ontiveros, Irene Fornes, Emilio Carballido, Susana Tubert, Toni Curiel, Jorge Huerta, Jon Mercedes III, Luis Valdez, Sara Valdovinos, Angelica López, Esther López, Teresa Marrero, Carmen Roman, INTAR, LATC, El Teatro De La Esperanza, University of California San Diego Theater Dept., The Guadalupe Cultural Arts Center, El Teatro Bilingue de Houston, The Seattle Group Theater, Asolo Center for the Performing Arts, Victory Gardens Theater, Dallas Theater Center, The San Diego Repertory Theater, Borderlands Theater, Repertorio Espanol and Spelman College.

PLAYWRIGHT'S NOTES

When I was very young my best friend and I were walking to the comer store. My parents had warned me not to tell anyone I didn't have "papers" and to be careful walking the streets. On the way to the store we saw "**la migra**" (INS/immigration/Border Patrol). I quickly turned to my friend and tried to "act white." I spoke in English and talked about Jordache jeans and Barbie dolls hoping no one would suspect us. When I finally got my legal residence card, I remembered this incident, knowing that I would never have to hide and be afraid again. I also laughed at my naiveté and fear because what I had thought was **la migra** was only the L.A. Police Meter Maid.

In 1987, the Simpson-Rodino Amnesty Law, designed to stop the influx of undocumented people entering the country, granted thousands of undocumented people living in the U.S. since 1982 legal residency. This was an opportunity of a lifetime. However, thousands, not trusting the government, hesitated to apply, fearing this was a scheme to deport them. They, like me, couldn't believe that after hiding and being persecuted for so long they were fmally going to have the freedom to live and work in this country.

I got my residence card soon after I graduated from high school and was then able to apply to college. I had been accepted to New York University, but I had to wait a year to be eligible for fmancial aid. During this year I worked at McDonald's, but I hated it. Then, desperate for a new job, I asked my sister to let me work at her tiny sewing factory. I worked there for five months and my experiences at the factory served as inspiration for *Real Women Have Curves*. At the factory there were a few Latina women, all older than me. They liked working for my sister because she wasn't stingy. We spent so much time together working, sweating and laughing, that we bonded. I remember feeling blessed that I was a woman because male bonding could never compare with what happens when women work together. We had something special and I wanted to show the world.

In the U.S. undocumented people are referred to as "illegal aliens," which conjures up in our minds the image of extraterrestrial beings who are not human, who do not bleed when they're cut, who do not cry when they feel pain, who do not have fears, dreams and hopes … Undocumented people have been used as scapegoats for so many of the problems in the U.S., from drugs and violence to the economy. I hope that someday this country recognizes the very important contributions of undocumented people and remembers that they too came to this country in search of a better life.

—Josefina López
Los Angeles
March, 1992

Real Women Have Curves

CHARACTERS

ANA: 18, plump and pretty, sister of Estela, daughter of Carmen. She is a recent high-school graduate and a young feminist who wants to go to college but is stuck in the factory helping out her sister.

ESTELA: 34, plump, plain-looking, owner of the "Garcia Sewing Factory," a hopeless romantic at heart, but a hard worker.

CARMEN: 50, a short, large woman, mother of Ana and Estela. She has a talent for storytelling and gossip.

PANCHA: 32, a huge woman who is very mellow in her ways, but quick with her tongue, very Catholic and traditional at times.

ROSALI: 29, thin, sweet and easygoing, but has a secret and is insecure about her sexual appeal.

VOICE OVER ONLY

ESPERANZA: 40s, female, a radio therapist with a talk show.

CALLER: 20s, an immigrant Latina who is experiencing domestic violence.

KLOVE RADIO HOST: male, a baritone voice with charm.

NIGHT SHIFT RADIO DJ: male, mellow voice.

NEWS RADIO REPORTER: male, Caucasian, with urgency in his voice.

SETTING

A tiny sewing factory in East Los Angeles.

NOTE: You will find a glossary of Spanish terms in the back of the book.

SCENES

ACT I

    Scene 1: Monday morning, August 7, 1987, about 7:00 a.m.

    Scene 2: A few hours later, about 11:30 a.m.

    Scene 3: A few hours later, about 3:45 p.m.

    Scene 4: The following day, about 7:10 a.m.

    Scene 5: Later the same day. Late afternoon.

ACT II

    Scene 1: Wednesday, August 9th, about 8:15 a.m.

    Scene 2: Thursday, August 10th, about 2:00 a.m.

    Scene 3: Same day, about 2:00 p.m.

    Scene 4: Friday, August 11th, about 2:25 p.m.

Real Women Have Curves

ACT I

SCENE 1

AT RISE: *Monday morning, August 7, about 7:00 a.m. The stage becomes visible. The clock on the wall shows it is 6:59 a.m. Keys are heard outside the door. The door opens. ANA and CARMEN enter. ANA drags herself in, goes directly to the electricity box and switches it on. Automatically all the machines "hummmm" loudly. The lights turn on at different times. The radio also blasts on with a song in Spanish. CARMEN quickly turns off the radio. She puts her lunch on the table. ANA slumps on a machine. CARMEN then gets a broom and uses it to get a mousetrap from underneath the table. She prays that today will be the day she caught the mouse. She sees the mousetrap empty and is very disappointed.*

CARMEN. ¡Pinche rata! I'll get you. *(Returns the broom. She takes two dollars from her purse, approaches ANA and presents them to her.)* Ten. Go to the bakery.

ANA. No. I want to go back to sleep!

CARMEN. ¡Huevona! If we don't help your sister who else is going to? She already works all hours of the night trying to finish the dresses. Por fin she's doing something productive with her life.

ANA. I know I'm trying to be supportive, ayy! I don't want to go to the bakery. I don't want any bread.

11

CARMEN. That's good, at least you won't get fatter.

ANA. ¡Amá!

CARMEN. I only tell you for your own good. Bueno, I'll go get the bread myself, but you better not get any when I bring it. *(CARMEN walks to the door.)* Ana, don't forget to close the doors. This street is full of winos and drug addicts. And don't you open the door to any strangers!

ANA. Yeah, yeah, I know! I'm not a kid. *(Locks both doors with a key. She goes toward the toilet and turns on the water in the sink. ANA splashes water on her face to awaken. She sticks her hand behind the toilet seat and gets out a notebook and a pen. Spotlight on ANA. She sits and writes the following:)* Monday August 7th … I don't want to be here! I only come because my mother practically drags me out of bed and into the car and into the factory. She pounds on the … No … *(Scratches "pounds.")* She knocks on … No … *(She scratches "knocks.")* She pounds on the garage wall, and since I think it's an earthquake, I run out. Then she catches me and I become her prisoner … Is it selfish of me not to want to wake up every morning at 6:30 a.m., Saturdays included, to come work here for 267 dollars a week? Oh, but such is the life of a Latina in the garment industry. Cheap labor … I've been trying to hint to my sister for a raise, but she says I don't work fast enough for her to pay me minimum wage … The weeks get longer and I can't believe I've ended up here. I just graduated from high school … Most of my friends are in college … It's as if I'm going backwards. I'm doing the work that mostly illegal aliens do … *(Scratches "illegal aliens.")* No, "undocumented workers" … or else it sounds like these people come from Mars … Soon I will have my "Temporary Residence Card," then after two years, my "Green card" … I'm happy to finally be legal, but I thought things would be different … What I really want to do is write …

CARMEN *(off, interrupting)*. Ana, open the door! *(CARMEN pounds on the door outside. ANA quickly puts her writing away and goes to open the door.)* Hurry up! There's a wino following me! *(ANA gets the keys and unlocks both doors.)* Hurry! He's been following me from the bakery.

(ANA opens the first door. CARMEN is behind the bar door and is impatiently waiting for ANA to open it. ANA opens the door. CARMEN hurries in nervously. ANA quickly shuts the doors. ANA looks out the window.)

ANA. Amá, that's not a wino, it's an "Alelullah"!

CARMEN. But he was following me!

ANA. I know, those "born agains" don't give up.

(CARMEN puts the bag of bread on the table. She fills a small pot with water and puts it on the little hot plate to boil the water for coffee.)

CARMEN. Pos yo ya no veo. I can't see a thing. *(CARMEN goes to her purse and takes out her glasses. She puts them on. She looks out the window and sees no one.)* I should retire and just be an abuelita by now, taking care of grandchildren … I don't know why I just work so much, I have arthritis in my hands, I'm losing my sight from all this sewing, and this arm, I can hardly move it anymore … *(ANA does not pay attention as usual.)*

ANA *(unsympathetically)*. Yeah, Amá.

CARMEN. I wonder where's Estela. She should have been here by now.

ANA. I thought she left the house early.

(PANCHA appears behind the bar door.)

PANCHA. Buenos días, Doña Carmen. Can you open the door?

CARMEN. Buenos días, Pancha. ¿Cómo está?

PANCHA. Not too bad.

CARMEN. Que bien. I brought my mole today for all of us.

PANCHA. You're so generous, Doña Carmen.

CARMEN. It was in the 'frigerator for three days, and I thought it was turning green, so I brought it. Why let it go to waste?

PANCHA. Is it still good?

CARMEN. Of course, I make great mole.

(ROSALI appears behind the bar door.)

ROSALI. Doña Carmen, the door.

CARMEN. It's open, Rosalí. Buenos días. How are you?

ROSALI *(entering)*. OK, like always, Doña Carmen.

CARMEN. I brought my mole for all of us.

ROSALI. Did you? Ayy, gracias, but remember I'm on a diet.

CARMEN. Just try a small taco, no te va hacer daño. Try it.

ROSALI. I'm sure it's delicious, but I'm this close to being a size two.

CARMEN. Sí. You're looking thinner now. How are you doing it?

ROSALI. I'm on a secret diet … It's from China.

CARMEN. A-ha … It's true, those Japanese women are always skinny. Pues, give me your secret, Rosalí. Maybe this way I can lose this ball of fat! *(She squeezes her stomach.)* No mas mira que paresco. You can't even see my waist anymore. But you know what it really is. It's just water. After having so many babies I just stopped getting rid of the water. It's like I'm clogged.

(ROSALI and ANA laugh.)

ROSALI. Sí, Doña Carmen.

ANA. Yeah, sure, Amá!

CARMEN. ¿Y tu? Why do you laugh? You're getting there yourself. When I was your age I wasn't as fat as you. And look at your chichis. *(Grabs ANA's breasts as if weighing them.)*

ANA. ¡Amá!

CARMEN. They must weigh five pounds each.

ANA. Amá, don't touch me like that!

ROSALI. Where's Estela?

CARMEN. We don't know. Ana, I think you better call home now and check if she's there.

ROSALI. Because her torment is outside washing his car.

ALL. He is?

(From under a large blanket on the floor ESTELA jumps out. The WOMEN are startled and scream, but they quickly join her as she runs to the window to spy on her Tormento.)

ESTELA. ¡Ayy que buenote! He's so cute.

ANA. Don't exaggerate.

ESTELA. ¡Mi Tormento! ¡O mi Tormento!

CARMEN. We thought you left home early.

ESTELA. No, I worked so late last night I decided to sleep here.

CARMEN. Then why didn't you tell us when—

ESTELA. I heard you come in, but I wanted to listen in on your chisme about me, Amá.

CARMEN. Me? I don't gossip!

ESTELA. Sure, Amá … I'm going to the store. *(Runs to the mirror.)*

PANCHA. I don't know why you bother, all he cares about is his car.

CARMEN. Vénganse, I think the water is ready.

(The WOMEN gather around the table for coffee. PANCHA and CARMEN grab bread. ESTELA goes to the bathroom and brushes her hair, puts on lipstick, then she puts on a girdle under her skirt, which she has great trouble getting on, but she is determined. She grabs a deodorant stick and applies it. She also gets a bottle of perfume and sprays it accordingly.)

ESTELA. Aquí por si me abraza. *(She sprays her wrist.)*

ANA *(mocks ESTELA in front of the WOMEN)*. Here in case he hugs me.

ESTELA. Aquí por si me besa. *(She sprays her neck.)*

ANA. Here in case he kisses me.

ESTELA. Y aquí por si se pasa. *(She sprays under her skirt.)*

ANA. And here in case he … you know what.

(The WOMEN are by the door and windows looking out. ESTELA comes out of the bathroom.)

ROSALI. He's gone.

CARMEN. Sí, ya se fue.

ESTELA. No! Are you sure?

(ESTELA goes toward the door. Before she reaches it, CARMEN shuts the door.)

CARMEN *(scared)*. ¡Dios mio! *(Quickly takes a drink of her coffee and can hardly breathe afterwards.)*

ESTELA. ¿Qué? ¿Amá, qué pasa?

CARMEN. I saw a van!

ROSALI. What van?

CARMEN. ¡La migra!

(All the WOMEN scatter and hide, waiting to be discovered. Then after a few seconds PANCHA makes a realization.)

PANCHA. Pero, why are we hiding? We're all legal now.

CARMEN. ¡Ayy, de veras! I forget! All those years of being sin papeles, I still can't get used to it.

PANCHA. Me too! *(She picks up a piece of bread.)* I think I just lost my appetite.

ROSALI. I'm not scared of it! I used to work in factories and whenever they did a raid, I'd always sneak out through the bathroom window, y ya.

ANA. Last night I heard on the news that I.C.E. is planning to raid a lot of places.

CARMEN: I.C.E.? What's that?

PANCHA. La Migra! They're going to get mean trying to enforce that new immigration law.

ANA. Thank God, I'm legal. I will never have to lie on applications anymore, except maybe about my weight …

ROSALI. ¿Saben qué? Yesterday I got my first credit card.

CARMEN. ¿Pos cómo le hiciste? How?

ROSALI. I lied on the application and I got an Americana Express.

ANA. And now you have two green cards and you never leave home without them.

(ANA laughs her head off, but none of the WOMEN get the joke. ANA slowly shuts up.)

PANCHA. Doña Carmen, let those men in their van come! Who cares? We're all legal now!

(PANCHA goes to the door and opens it all the way. They all smile in relief and pride, then ESTELA, who has been stuffing her face, finally speaks up.)

ESTELA. I'm not. *(PANCHA slams the door shut.)*

EVERYONE. You're not?!!!

ANA. But you went with me to get the fingerprints and the medical examination.

ESTELA. I didn't send them in.

ROSALI. But you qualify.

ESTELA. I have a criminal record.

EVERYONE. No!

ESTELA. So I won't apply until I clear it.

CARMEN. Estela, what did you do?

PANCHA. ¿Qué hiciste?

ESTELA. Well, actually, I did two things.

CARMEN. Two?! ¿Y por qué no me habias dicho? Why is the mother always the last one to know?

ESTELA. Because one is very embarrassing—

CARMEN. ¡Aver dime, condenada! What have you done?

ESTELA. I was arrested for illegal possession of—

ROSALI. Marijuana?!

PANCHA. A gun?!

ESTELA. A lobster.

EVERYONE. No!

ESTELA. Out of season!

CARMEN. ¡Mentirosa!

WOMEN. You're kidding!

ESTELA. A-ha! I'm not lying! I almost got handcuffed and taken to jail. Trying to "abduct" a lobster is taken very seriously in Santa Monica Beach. They wanted me to appear in court and I never did.

PANCHA. That's not a serious crime; ¿de qué te apuras? Why worry?

CARMEN *(not amused)*. That was the first crime? You mentioned two.

ESTELA. I'm being sued for not keeping up with my payments on the machines.

ANA. Y los eight thousand dollars you got from your accident settlement weren't enough?

CARMEN. But I thought that everything was paid for.

ESTELA. I used most of it for a down-payment, but I still needed a new steam iron, the over-lock … I thought I could make the monthly payments if everything went as planned.

CARMEN. ¿Pos qué paso?

PANCHA. What happened?

ESTELA. You know that we never finish on time. So the Glitz company doesn't pay me until we do.

ROSALI. Pero the orders are too big. We need at least two more seamstresses.

ESTELA. Pues sí. But the money they pay me is not enough to hire any more help. So because we get behind, they don't pay, I can't pay you, and I can't pay those pigs that sold me those machines.

CARMEN. Ayyy, Estela, how much do you owe?

ESTELA. Ten thousand dollars…

CARMEN. ¡Hora si que estamos bien jodidas!

(The WOMEN sigh hopelessly.)

ESTELA. ... I tried. I sent some money and explained the situation to them two weeks ago, but I got a letter from their lawyer. They're taking me to court ...

PANCHA. So you had money two weeks ago? Hey, hey, you told us you couldn't pay us because you didn't have any money. You had money! Here we are bien pobres, I can't even pay for the bus sometimes, and you care more about your machines than us.

ESTELA. They're going to take everything!

ROSALI. ¡¿Qué?!

ESTELA. They're going to repossess everything if I don't pay them. And if I appear in court they'll find out that I don't have any papers.

ANA. Estela, you should talk to this lawyer I know ...

ESTELA. Ana, you know I can't afford a lawyer!

CARMEN. Ayy, Estela, ¡ya ni la friegas!

(ESTELA fights the urge to cry.)

ROSALI. If I had money I'd lend it to you.

PANCHA *(aside)*. I wouldn't.

ROSALI *(kindly)*. But I don't have any money because you haven't paid me.

ESTELA. Miren, the Glitz company has promised to pay me for the last two weeks and this week if we get the order in by Friday.

ANA. How much of the order is left?

ESTELA. About 100 dresses.

PANCHA. N'ombre. By this Friday? What do they think we are? Machines?

ESTELA. But they're not that difficult! Amá, you're so fast. This would be a cinch for you. All you have to do are the blusas on the dresses. Rosalí, the over-lock work is simple. It's a lot, but you're the best at it. And, Pancha, all you have to do is sew the skirts. The skirts are the easiest to sew. Now, Ana, with you doing all the ironing, we'll get it done by Friday. You see if we do little by little at what we do best … ¡Andenle! We can do it. ¿Verá que sí, Ana?

ANA *(uncertain)*. Sure we can.

ESTELA. ¿Vera que sí, Amá?

CARMEN. Pos we can try.

ROSALI. Estela, we can do it.

(ESTELA looks to PANCHA. PANCHA remains quiet. CARMEN breaks their stare.)

CARMEN. Wouldn't it be funny if the migra came and instead of taking the employees like they usually do, they take the patrona.

(The WOMEN laugh at the thought.)

ESTELA. Don't laugh! It could happen.

(The WOMEN become silent.)

CARMEN. Ayy, Estela, I'm just kidding. I'm just trying to make you feel better.

(Beat.)

ROSALI. Bueno, let's try to be serious … I'll do the zippers.

ESTELA. Yes, por favor. And, Pancha, please do the hems on the skirts.

PANCHA. The machine is not working.

ESTELA. Not again! *(Goes to the machine. She fusses around with it trying to make it work. With confidence.)* There. It should be ready. Try it.

(PANCHA sits down on a chair and tries the machine. She steps on the pedal and the machine makes an awful noise. Then it shoots off electric sparks and explodes. PANCHA quickly gets away from the machine. The WOMEN hide under the machines.)

WOMEN. ¡Ay, ay, ay!

ESTELA. Augghh! All this equipment is junk! *(Throws a thread spool at the machine and it explodes again.)* I was so stupid to buy this factory!

(ESTELA fights the urge to cry in frustration. The WOMEN stare at her helplessly.)

CARMEN. Pos no nos queda otra. Pancha, can you do the hems by hand?

PANCHA. Bueno, I guess I have to.

ESTELA. Gracias … Ana, turn on the iron, I'm going to need you to do the ironing all this week … Tell me when the iron gets hot and I'll show you what you have to do.

CARMEN. I'll help Rosalí with the zippers.

ESTELA. No … I need you to do the blusas on size 8.

CARMEN. Didn't I already do them?

ESTELA. No.

CARMEN. I guess it was size 14 then.

ESTELA. You couldn't have, because there is no size 14 for this dress style, Amá.

CARMEN. No? … Hoye did you get any more pink thread from the Glitz?

ESTELA. Oh, no. I forgot … Go ahead and use the over-lock machine. That is already set up with thread.

ANA. What does the over-lock do?

ROSALI. It's what keeps the material from coming apart. *(Shows* ANA.)

CARMEN. Why don't you give me the pink thread from the over-lock machine, then when you get the thread you can set it up again?

ESTELA. No. I don't know how to set it up on that new machine.

CARMEN. Rosalí can do that later. She knows how to do it; qué no, Rosalí?

ROSALI. Sí, Doña Carmen.

ESTELA. Why don't you just do what I'm asking you to do?

CARMEN. Estela, no seas terca. I know what I'm telling you.

ESTELA. So do I. I want to do things differently. I want us to work like an assembly line.

CARMEN. Leave that to the big factories. I've been working long enough to know—

ESTELA. I haven't been working long enough, but I'm intelligent enough to—

CARMEN. Estela, my way is better!

ESTELA. Why do you think your way is better? All my life your way has been better. Maybe that's why my life is so screwed up!

CARMEN. ¡Desgraciada! I'm only doing it to help you!

ESTELA. Because you know I won't be getting married any time soon so you want to make sure I'm doing something productive with my life so I can support myself. I don't need your help! *(Beat.)*

CARMEN. Where did all that come from? I thought we were arguing about the thread.

ESTELA. You know what I mean. You know I'm right!

CARMEN. All right. If you want me to do the over-lock work I'll do it … I have to remember I work for you now.

ESTELA. Amá, don't give me that!

CARMEN. What?

ESTELA. Guilt!

CARMEN. Well, it's true! It's not usual that a mother works for her daughter. So I have to stop being your mother and just be a regular employee that you can boss around and tell what to do.

ESTELA. ¡Ayy, Amá, parele! You are my mother, but sometimes you get out of line. How can I tell Rosalí and Pancha to stop gossiping when it's you who initiates the chisme? You're a bad example!

CARMEN. Ay, sí. Blame me! ¡Echame la culpa! You gossip too when it's convenient.

ESTELA. Look, Amá, I don't want to argue with you anymore. I'm frustrated enough by the thought that I might get deported, at the sight of that machine, and at the thought that I am the biggest pendeja for buying all this junk. So I don't need my mother to make my life any worse!

(Beat.)

CARMEN. So what are we going to do about the thread?

ESTELA. ¡Oiiiii! And we're back to the same thing! *(She goes to the over-lock machine and angrily tears a thread spool from the machine and throws it at CARMEN.)* Here! ¡Tenga!

(The thread spool misses CARMEN by a hair.)

CARMEN *(dramatically).* ¡Pegame, pegame! Go ahead! Hit me! God's gonna punish you for enojona!

ANA. Estela, the iron is ready.

ESTELA. Amá, give me a finished dress from the box.

CARMEN. Where are they?

ESTELA. Right next to you by the pile.

CARMEN. Qué size?

ESTELA. For the mannequin.

CARMEN. What size is it?

ROSALI. It's a size two, Doña Carmen.

CARMEN *(sarcastically).* Thank you, Rosali.

(CARMEN digs into the box and gets a dress. She gives it to ESTELA who begins to iron the dress carefully.)

ESTELA *(to ANA).* Pay close attention to how I'm ironing this dress. Always, always use the steam. And don't burn the tul, por favor. On the skirt just a couple of strokes to make it look decent. It's real easy, just don't burn the tulle, OK?

ANA. OK.

ESTELA. Check the water, and when it gets low … Tell me so I can send you to buy some more water for it.

ANA. Why do you have to buy the water?

ESTELA. Because regular water is too dirty, it needs distilled water for clean steam.

(ESTELA finishes ironing the dress. She shakes it a bit then puts it on the mannequin. All the WOMEN stare at the dress.)

ROSALI. Que bonito. How I would like to wear a dress like that.

PANCHA. But first you have to turn into a stick to wear something like that.

ROSALI. Yeah, but they're worth it.

ANA. How much do they pay us for making these dresses?

ESTELA. Ah, let me see, these are silk charmeuse. For these we get thirty dollars a dress.

ANA. Oh, yeah? How much do they sell them for at the stores?

ESTELA. They tell me they sell them at Bloomingdale's for about four hundred dollars.

WOMEN. ¡¡¿Qué?!!

ANA. Dang!!

(Lights fade.)

SCENE 2

(A few hours later, about 11:30 a.m. Lights come on. The WOMEN are busy working. ANA stops ironing for a few seconds. She pulls out her cellphone from her backpack, trying not to be spotted. ESTELA sees her on her cell.)

ESTELA. Ana, what does that say?

(ESTELA points to the poster that says "Gossipping is Prohibited.")

ANA. I'm not going to gossip, I'm just going to check my Instagram—

ESTELA. No cellphones allowed. You know that, now put it away.

(ANA rolls her eyes at ESTELA and puts her cellphone away. The "Cucaracha" is played on the horn by the lunch mobile outside announcing its arrival.)

ANA. OK, there's the lonchera. Anybody want anything for lunch?

CARMEN. The lonchera is here already?

ESTELA. Ana, just hurry back.

ROSALI. Can you get me something to drink? How much are those tomato juices?

ANA. A V-8?

ROSALI. Sí, eso.

ANA. I think they're $1.78. You want anything else?

ROSALI. No, no, I'm not hungry.

ESTELA. Ana, lend me three dollars.

ANA. What do you think I am? A bank? This is the third time. One can only go so far on 267 dollars a week.

ESTELA. Ana, if you are not happy here go back to working at McDonald's.

ANA. I would … *(CARMEN stares at ANA.)* … But … You still want to borrow the three dollars?

ESTELA. Are you going to charge me interest?

ANA. Of course. What do you want me to buy you?

ESTELA. A burrito de chicharrón.

ANA. Pancha, do you want anything?

PANCHA. Sí. Bring me four tacos.

CARMEN. Pancha, aren't you going to want some of my mole?

PANCHA. Ana, bring me three tacos, no más.

(PANCHA gives ANA money.)

ESTELA. Ana, if you have money left, could you buy some distilled water at the corner store?

ANA. Anything else, boss?

(ANA leaves to buy the food. CARMEN waits until ESTELA shuts the door.)

CARMEN. Bueno, if we are already going to hell for being a bunch of chismosas, there's no use in hiding it any longer. *(CARMEN digs into a pile of dresses and takes out a book. She shows it to PANCHA and ROSALI. CARMEN whispers.)* ¡Miren!

(ROSALI quickly sees the illustrations on the front cover and is shocked.)

ROSALI. Doña Carmen!

CARMEN. I was cleaning the garage and I found a whole pile of dirty books. I think they belonged to my oldest son.

PANCHA. What's the book called?

ROSALI *(reading title).* Two Hundred Sexual Positions Illustrated.

PANCHA. I didn't know there were so many.

(ROSALI and PANCHA gather around CARMEN to look at the book. ESTELA has not noticed them. Instead she notices a letter being dropped in the mail slot. ESTELA reads the letter.)

ROSALI *(shocked).* Ay, Dios, how can these women do this?

PANCHA. They're probably gymnasts.

CARMEN. The photographer must have used a special lens on this picture.

PANCHA. Which picture?

CARMEN. The one on page 69.

ROSALI. I didn't know people could do that.

PANCHA. ¡Híjole! Imagine if you had married this man, and you had never seen him until your wedding night.

CARMEN. ¡N'ombre, ni lo mande dios! How it hurt with a regular one.

PANCHA. Mire, Doña Carmen. This woman looks like you, but that doesn't stop her.

CARMEN. Ahh. She's so big. No le da verguenza.

ROSALI. I didn't know they had large women in porno books.

PANCHA. I guess some men enjoy watching big women.

ESTELA (sees them looking at the book). What are you looking at? You're suppose to be working! The food has not gotten here yet.

PANCHA. Estela, come look. It's a dirty book.

ESTELA. Why are you looking at that?

CARMEN. Estela, no mas ven a ver.

(ESTELA hesitates, but is curious and gives in. She sees the pictures of the large women and is shocked.)

ESTELA. People this fat shouldn't be having sex! Ichhh!

ROSALI. Look, Estela, there's a guy in here that looks like your "Tormento."

ESTELA. Where?!! (ROSALI shows her, then suddenly the door is kicked open.) Aughhhhhh!!!!!

(ANA enters with her hands full of food.)

PANCHA. Estela, calm down.

ESTELA. I thought it was la migra!

ANA. Sorry! I kicked the door open because my hands are full …

ESTELA. From now on these doors are to remain closed and locked at all times, OK? If you go outside, you knock on the door like this … *(She knocks in code rhythm.)* … so we know it's just one of us. Don't ever kick the door again.

ANA. Isn't that going a bit to extremes?

PANCHA. Vamos a estar como gallinas enjauladas.

ESTELA. No. We just have to be careful.

ROSALI. So how do you do the knock?

ESTELA *(exemplifies)*. Knock once. Pause. Then knock twice. Then repeat.

ANA. Well, if it makes you feel better …

ESTELA. Yes, it would.

ANA. All right. Here's the food.

(ANA places the food on the table.)

ESTELA. Did you remember the water?

ANA. Yeah, I brought the water! *(ANA gives the bottle of water to ESTELA and distributes the food. To the WOMEN:)* What were you doing?

ALL *(hiding the book)*. Nothin'.

ANA. What are you hiding?

ALL. Nothin'. *(Pause.)*

PANCHA. We don't want to pervert you.

ANA. You don't want to pervert me more than I've already perverted you?

ROSALI. It's a dirty book.

ANA. Let me see it.

CARMEN. No! You're too young to be looking at these things.

ANA. Fine. You've seen them once, you've seen it all.

PANCHA. Ana!

CARMEN. ¿Qué? Repeat what you just said. Don't tell me you've been "messing around."

ANA. No. It's just that I probably know more than most of you and you're thinking that you can pervert me. Stuupid!!!

CARMEN. And how is it that you know so much if you haven't done it?

ANA. ... I read a lot.

PANCHA. But not because you read a lot means you know what's what.

ANA. Go ahead. Ask me anything you always wanted to know about sex but were afraid to ask. I'll tell you.

(All the WOMEN are tempted.)

ROSALI. How do you masturbate ... ?

(PANCHA, CARMEN, and ESTELA stare at ROSALI in shock.)

ANA. What?

CARMEN. ¡Híjole! If your Apá were to hear you ... ¡Híjole!

ANA. I wouldn't be talking like this in front of my father.

CARMEN. Can you believe her? Girls nowadays think they know so much that's why they end up panzonas.

ANA. No. They end up pregnant because they don't use contraceptives.

PANCHA. Are you sure all you do is read a lot?

CARMEN. Your husband's not going to like you knowing so much.

PANCHA. A girl shouldn't know so much.

ANA. I'm not a girl, I'm a woman.

PANCHA. Uuy, uy, la Miss Know-it-all.

CARMEN. In my day, a girl became a woman when she lost her virginity.

ANA. That was then. I read somewhere that calling someone a "girl" is just as bad as when white men used to call black men—

CARMEN *(starts to laugh uncontrollably)*. I ... I ... remember ...

ESTELA. Amá, it's 12:20, no more stories. If we gossip people are gonna hear everything outside and even if we close the doors they'll know it's a sewing factory because only women talking chisme can sound like chickens cackling.

CARMEN. But it's what I know how to do best, my reason for living.

ESTELA. I'm begging you.

(CARMEN remains quiet for a few seconds then she begins to laugh uncontrollably again.)

PANCHA. Why are you laughing? *(CARMEN continues laughing, unable to speak.)*

ANA. ¿Amá, qué le píco?

(The laughter is contagious.)

CARMEN. I just got a back flash of when I lost my virginity.

ANA. That bad, huh?

CARMEN. The night I eloped with your father on his bicycle ...

ESTELA. Bueno, if the migra deports me we know whose fault it is. Amá, no work, no money, no factory! Is that clear enough?!

CARMEN. Pero, don't get upset. Estela, it's lunch time.

PANCHA. Pues sí.

ESTELA. It gets me so annoyed to hear her talk and talk … And with all the work we have! Just promise me that you'll finish, all right? I'll stop bothering you if you can do that.

WOMEN *(look to each other)*. Pues bueno. We promise.

ESTELA. If not you'll go to hell?!

WOMEN *(look to each other again and think about it)*. Pues bueno.

CARMEN. Sí, sí, sí, we'll go to hell. Can I continue? OK, pues after riding on his bike for so long, I had to pee so bad! So we stopped in the mountains somewhere. I ran behind a tree, squatted, and just peed. That night, after we got settled, I didn't know what was going to happen. After we did it, I started itching and scratching down there till my cuchupeta got so red. I thought something was wrong, but I asked him and he said it was suppose to hurt and bleed. Then I found out it wasn't him. I had peed on poison ivy. And how it hurt! *(The WOMEN laugh sympathetically and slowly gather around the table to eat.)* Panchita, try some of my mole.

PANCHA *(looking at mole)*. But, Doña Carmen, it's green.

CARMEN. It's green mole … Ana, you didn't try some mole. It's real good.

ANA. No way! It looks like … yukkkk!

CARMEN. Aver, Rosalí, come try some. There's plenty.

ROSALI. Thank you, pero, I'm not hungry.

CARMEN. But you haven't eaten anything.

ROSALI. I drink eight glasses of water a day and I don't feel hungry. Water gets rid of the fat.

CARMEN. Ana, you should be drinking eight waters.

ANA. And you should too … Oh no, you get clogged.

ESTELA. Amá, just be very careful with the mole. I don't want any of the dresses getting stained.

(PANCHA scoops some mole with a piece of tortilla. She eats the scoop.)

CARMEN. You like it, Pancha?

PANCHA *(lying)*. Yeah, it's real good, Doña Carmen …

(ROSALI carefully strays away from the table and drinks her V-8. ROSALI swallows a pill. She goes to the window and peeks out through the curtain. She spots el Tormento outside.)

ROSALI. ¡Míralo! There's Andrés! Estela, come to the window! Your Tormento is outside!

(PANCHA, CARMEN, and ANA run to the window, beating ESTELA.)

ESTELA. No, don't go to the window! Get away from the window.

ANA. No one can see us!

ESTELA. Get down! Make some room for me!

CARMEN. I don't see what you could possibly see in him.

ESTELA. He's cute and he likes me.

CARMEN. He doesn't even have good nalgas. They're this small.

(She exemplifies with her hands.)

ANA. Amá, why are you so preoccupied with the size of a man's butt?

ROSALI. That's not what counts.

CARMEN. Because your father doesn't have any nalgas.

(ESTELA goes to the door and opens it. She fixes herself a bit and stands in front of the door.)

PANCHA. Estela, I thought you said that door was going to remain closed.

ROSALI. Estela, get away from the door, because if the van passes they'll just see the nopal on your forehead and take you away.

ESTELA. But he wants to talk to me. He wrote me a letter.

(ESTELA leaves, closing the door.)

ANA. A letter? That's so old fashioned.

ROSALI. Wow. That's so romantic! That's better than getting a dumb text.

PANCHA. What man sends a letter these days?

CARMEN. Not like in our day when we waited weeks for a letter to come from el norte.

(CARMEN and PANCHA are still eating their tacos. They all go to the window and stick to the window like flies.)

CARMEN. What could he be telling her? She's laughing her head off.

ROSALI. ¡Miren cómo coquetea! What a flirt. You never suspected she had it in her.

PANCHA. She's worse than Ana.

ANA. What's that suppose to mean?

(CARMEN holds her taco carelessly and the mole spills out onto some dresses.)

PANCHA. ¡Mire, Doña Carmen! You're spilling the mole!

ANA. Amá, Estela is going to kill you!

CARMEN. ¡Ayy, no! *(Quickly puts the taco on the table. She grabs a cloth and tries to clean the dresses.)*

PANCHA. ¡Aguas! Here she comes!

CARMEN. What am I going to do?

ANA *(runs to the door and locks it)*. Quick, Amá. Hide the dresses! We'll clean them later.

CARMEN. ¿Dónde los escondo?

ROSALI. Anywhere!

(ESTELA tries to open the door. While the women run around hysterically trying to find the best place to hide the dresses.)

ESTELA. Let me in.

ANA. Who is it?

ESTELA. You know who it is!

ANA. I don't know who. *(She gestures to the women to hurry.)* You think we should open the door? What if it's I.C.E.?

ESTELA. Ana, open the door! *(She pounds on the door.)*

ANA. How do we know it's you?

(ESTELA finally knocks the secret code and ANA lets her in.)

ESTELA. When the cat is away the mice come out to play. What were you doing?

WOMEN. Nothing!

CARMEN. Ahora sí. Show us the letter first, and tell us what you talked about.

ESTELA. It's private.

ROSALI. Come on, Estela, no te hagas de rogar, you know you want to show it to us.

ESTELA. ¡Que metiches! This letter is for me. He only intended for me to read it … All right, I'll read it out loud. *(The WOMEN pull out their chairs and get comfortable. ESTELA clears her throat and reads the letter dramatically.)* "Dear Estela … " *(The WOMEN get excited after the first "Dear.")* "Dear Estela … How I dig you. Let me count the waves."

ROSALI. Ahhh, it's a poem.

ESTELA. "Wave one: 'cause you look real nice when you pass by me and say, 'Hi.' Wave two: 'cause you seem real smart. Wave three: 'cause your eyes are like fresas. And your lips are like mangos, juicy and delicious, listos para chupar."

PANCHA. Maybe he works at the supermarket in the fruit section.

ESTELA *(continues)*. "So how about it? You wanna go cruising down Whittier Boulevard, see a movie, or anything else you wanna do?" I told him I liked the letter a lot. So we're going to the movies tonight.

ROSALI. To the movies? It sounds serious. But be careful with those wandering hands.

ESTELA. He's not that kind of guy.

CARMEN. So what are you going to wear? Don't go dressing up like a scarecrow now.

ESTELA. I don't dress like that.

CARMEN. That's why you scare them away.

ESTELA. Como es, Amá. He likes me for me. Didn't you hear? He said I'm intelligent. He doesn't care how I dress.

CARMEN. Estela, let me make you a dress, horitita te lo coso.

ESTELA. No. I can dress myself. And anyway, what are we doing sitting around. Lunch is over. Let's get to work. ¡A trabajar!

(Lights fade out.)

SCENE 3

(A few hours later, about 3:45 p.m. Lights fade in. The WOMEN are busy working in their designated working areas. PANCHA is by the racks attaching strings to hang the dresses.)

ANA. Estela, there are no more dresses to iron. What else should I do?

ESTELA. Ah ... Pancha, can you show Ana what you are doing?

(ANA goes to the racks. ROSALI turns on the radio.)

PANCHA *(showing ANA)*. Hazlo Asi. This way.

(ANA quickly understands what she has to do and begins her work. ESTELA's cellphone rings. ESTELA picks it up. On the radio we hear the following:)

RADIO *(V.O.)*. It's 3:45 and it's already 99 degrees—another hot, beautiful day in L.A. This is KLOVE—Radio Amor ... Now back to our talk show, "Esperanza."

ESPERANZA *(V.O.)*. For those of you who just joined us today we are discussing abusive spouses. We have our last caller on the line. Caller, are you there?

CALLER *(V.O.)*. Hi. I'm not going to give you my name because my husband listens to this station. I wanted to know what I can do to ... Well, I want to know how I can talk to my husband when he gets angry.

ESPERANZA *(V.O.)*. How long has he been abusive?

CALLER *(V.O.)*. Ah … Well, he wasn't like this when we got married … He was always sweet. So I don't know what has happened to him. He tells me if I did whatever he asked he wouldn't have to hit me. But I do what he says and it's still not good enough. Last time he hit me because …

PANCHA *(switches the dial on the radio)*. Isn't there anything else?

CARMEN. Pobre mujer, I'm lucky mi viejo doesn't hit me.

ANA. Lucky? Why lucky? It should be expected that he doesn't. That woman should leave her husband. Women have the right to say "no."

PANCHA. You think it's that easy?

ANA. No, she's probably dependent on him financially, or the church tells her to endure, or she's doing it for the children.

PANCHA. You're so young. Did it ever occur to you that maybe she loves him?

ANA. I'm sure she does. But we can't allow ourselves to be abused anymore. We have to assert ourselves. We have to realize that we have rights! We have the right to control our bodies. The right to exercise our sexuality. And the right to take control of our destiny. But it all begins when we start saying … *(ANA quickly climbs on top of a sewing machine to continue preaching.)* … ¡Ya basta! No more! We should learn how to say no! Come on, Amá, say it! Say it!

CARMEN. What?

ANA. Say it! "No!"

CARMEN. OK, I won't.

ANA. Amá, say "No!"

CARMEN *(as in she won't)*. No.

ANA. Good! Rosalí, say it.

ROSALI *(casually)*. ¿Pues por qué no? No.

ANA. Pancha, say it. No!

(PANCHA stares at ANA, she won't say it.)

ESTELA. Ya, ya, Norma Rae, get off and get back to work!

PANCHA. Why don't you run for office? Tan pequeña and she thinks and acts like she knows everything.

ANA. I don't know everything, but I know a lot. I read a lot. But it just amazes me to hear you talk the way you do. A women's liberation movement happened so long ago, and you act like it hasn't even happened.

PANCHA. Mira, all those gringas shouting about liberation hasn't done a thing for me … And if you were married you would realize it. Bueno, and if you know so much how come you're not in college?

ANA. Because I don't have the money. I have to wait a year to be eligible for financial aid.

PANCHA. I always thought that if you were smart enough a college would give you a scholarship. Maybe you should read some more and get one so you don't have to be here making 267 dollars a week and hearing us talk the way we do. *(A car honking is heard outside.)*

CARMEN. Ya llegó mi viejo. Ana, get ready. ¡Vámonos!

ANA. No, Amá, you go. I'll take the bus … I want to finish this last pile.

CARMEN. You do? Ah, I know why you want to stay, metiche. Bueno. Adiós.

WOMEN. Adiós.

(CARMEN leaves. PANCHA collects her belongings. A car honking is heard outside.)

PANCHA. I'm leaving too.

ROSALI. Pancha, do you want a ride?

PANCHA. Sí, sí. *(They get ready to leave.)*

ROSALI. Adiós, Estela. Good luck on your date with your Tormento. Well, not too good. I hope you won't need to go to confession tomorrow. *(ROSALI and ESTELA giggle.)* Hasta mañana.

(They leave. Soon after ESTELA finishes her call on her cellphone.)

ANA. So who was that?

ESTELA. María … She called to wish me a happy birthday.

ANA. Isn't it this Friday?

ESTELA. Yes, but she couldn't wait to tell me that she's getting married in three months. She wants me to make her wedding dress. *(They continue working.)* Ana, before el Tormento gets here you have to leave.

ANA. Why?

ESTELA. Because I don't want you writing about it. I know what you do in the bathroom.

ANA. Come on, Estela, where else can I write? I come here and all it is, is "work, work, work" from you and Amá. I go home and then she still wants me to help her cook, and clean …

ESTELA. So what are you writing?

ANA. I'm keeping a journal so when I become "rich and famous" I can write my autobiography.

ESTELA. Ana, who do you think you are? "Rich and famous."

ANA. I'm not going to be stuck here forever.

ESTELA. And I am?

ANA. No … I didn't say that. Amá y Apá, always said that you wouldn't do anything with your life, but you're proving them wrong. It takes a lot of guts and courage to do what you're doing. And even if you're in a mess, you have your own business, at 34! I'm very proud of you.

ESTELA *(a little embarrassed).* All right, Ana, you can stay.

ANA. So when is el Tormento picking you up?

ESTELA. In a few minutes. I won't even have a chance to freshen up. *(Goes to the sink and washes her face. She stares at herself in the mirror.)* Ana, do you have any makeup?

ANA. Not with me.

ESTELA *(continues to stare at herself with an excited face).* I don't have anything to wear!

(ESTELA runs to look for clothes to wear. ANA goes to the bathroom and sits on the toilet and begins to write. Spotlight on ANA.)

ANA. Another day and we're in deep … trouble … I keep having arguments with Pancha, and even though she doesn't like me, I feel sort of sorry for her. I wish I could tell her what to do, but she won't listen to me. Like the rest of the women, she won't take me seriously. They make fun of me … So why do I stay? … It's true. I stay. Because no matter how much my mother could try and force me to come, I could decide not to come back. But I do … Why?

(Fade out.

Lights come on. ESTELA is holding the pink dress. She looks to the bathroom to see if ANA is watching. She then holds the dress to her body as if wearing it. She dances slowly with it, imagining herself dancing with el Tormento. Lights slowly fade.)

SCENE 4

(The following day, Tuesday, about 7:10 a.m. Lights come on after a brief pause. On the calendar it is Tuesday. On the clock it is 7:10 a.m. Before the lights are fully on, ESTELA's crying is heard. The WOMEN are gathered around her.)

ANA. So what happened?!

ESTELA. He … He …

PANCHA. What did he do?

ESTELA. He … He …

ROSALI & ANA. What?!!

ESTELA. I don't want to talk about it! *(She pulls herself together.)* Let's forget about it and get started on the work … Amá, you said you were going to the bakery.

CARMEN. Ah, sí, sí.

ESTELA. Rosalí, how are you doing with the zippers?

ROSALI. I'm halfway done.

ESTELA. Ana, turn on the iron. There are a lot more dresses that need ironing. Pancha, are you almost done with the skirts for size 4?

PANCHA. No. I just started that lot a few minutes before I left yesterday.

CARMEN. Does anybody want anything from the bakery?

ESTELA. I want a juice … Ana, could you … ?

(ESTELA decides to look in her purse instead. She takes out all of her pennies and gives them to CARMEN.)

CARMEN. Estela, you can tell me. What could he have possibly done to get you this upset?

ESTELA. You're so stubborn, Amá! I said nothing happened. I'm just over-reacting.

CARMEN. Just remember, I'm your mother. If you can't trust your mother, who can you trust? *(The WOMEN agree with CARMEN, but ESTELA does not give in. CARMEN leaves. Quickly after, before ANA has a chance to lock the door, CARMEN runs back in and leans on the door to close it with her body. She is breathing heavily.)* It's out there again! Like a vulture!

PANCHA. What?

ALL. ¡La migra! *(They gasp. They all close the curtains and bolt the doors.)*

ROSALI. Was it going by slow or was it going by fast?

CARMEN. It was going slow like it was going to turn at the corner and circle around the block and come back!

ANA. You don't know that for sure!

CARMEN. Estela, it just occurred to me. Why don't you go home and work in the garage on our old sewing machine?

ESTELA. I could do that. But I can't. I don't trust you.

ROSALI. We'll work. Just go! ¡Rápido!

ESTELA. And you'll work?

ALL. Yes!!

ESTELA. What should I take with me to work on?

ROSALI. Just go! I'll get my Jaime to take you the work. Go!

ESTELA. OK! *(ESTELA begins to leave. She opens the door.)* He's out there! *(ESTELA runs to the bathroom.)*

ANA. Who? The man in the van?

PANCHA. No. ¡El Tormento!

ROSALI. Estela, come out of there! Go before they come. ¡Por favor!

CARMEN. Estela, get out of there right now! ¡No seas mensa! Men are not worth crying over. And they're certainly not worth you getting deported. *(CARMEN waits for ESTELA to come out.)* Vas a verlo. ¡Entonces a la fuerza! *(CARMEN pulls on the curtain and tries to drag ESTELA out. ESTELA wraps herself with the curtain and CARMEN is unable to get her out.)*

ESTELA. No! Leave me alone! I'm not coming out!

ANA. Estela, who's that gringa he's kissing? *(The curtain flies open and ESTELA races to the door.)*

ESTELA. Who?!! Where?!!

ANA. I lied. Now go home!

(ANA pushes ESTELA out the door and locks it. Beat.)

ROSALI *(looking out of the window)*. I don't think they're coming.

PANCHA. Are you sure you saw it, Doña Carmen?

ANA. They would have been here by now. ¿Qué no?

CARMEN. I guess so ... I don't understand.

(They sigh in relief.)

ESTELA *(offstage, knocking on the door)*. Ana, let me in.

(ESTELA knocks on the door and ANA finally lets her in.)

ESTELA *(cont'd)*. I'm going to stay.

CARMEN. All right.

(ESTELA closes the door, locks it. The WOMEN begin working; machines roar.)

ANA. Shit! I wish we had a fan here. *(Turns on the radio.)*
ESTELA. I don't want the dresses getting dirty with the dust.

(Lights fade.)

SCENE 5

(Later the same day. Late afternoon. Lights come on. The WOMEN are busy working. ANA goes to the bathroom. She sits on the toilet and starts writing in her journal.

Spotlight on ANA.)

ANA. It feels just as bad as when I was doing the fries at McDonald's. Pouring frozen sticks of potatoes into boiling lard and the steam hitting my face for minimum wage … This place stinks! I hate going to the store and having to climb over the winos, and ignore the catcalls of the sexist drug addicts and the smell of urine and marijuana on the street, and … I went to the store today and I saw an old friend. She's pregnant, again. She says she's happy and she doesn't care if she's on welfare. When she was still in high school she told me she knew I was going to do something with my life. I don't want her to know I work here.

(Lights come back on. The WOMEN shift in their chairs, uncomfortable with the heat in their buttocks. ROSALI fans herself and notices that CARMEN has an odd facial expression.)

ROSALI. Doña Carmen, why do you have that strange look on your face?
CARMEN. I reached over to get the next dress and I felt something moving inside. I think I'm pregnant.

PANCHA. Don't say that, Doña Carmen, or I'll lose faith in God. You're almost 50 and already have eight children, I'm barely 32 and can't have any.

CARMEN. Isn't that odd, I'm suppose to be an abuelita by now. Pero no puede ser, it can't be.

ESTELA. Amá, don't tell me you still have sex? At your age and in your physical condition?

ANA. Cállense, I heard something on the news about a raid.

(The WOMEN listen to the radio.)

RADIO *(V.O.)*. KNXW News all the time … The time now is 2:35 p.m. The temperature is scorching hot. A record breaking 102 degrees. Twenty illegal aliens were captured today at the Goodnight pillow factory …

PANCHA. That's only a few blocks away!

RADIO *(V.O.)*. I.C.E. was given a tip by anonymous sources yesterday of the factory's illegal hiring of aliens. The owner was fined up to 2,000 dollars per alien …

(PANCHA, CARMEN, and ROSALI do the sign of the holy cross.)

CARMEN. Estela, why don't you call the Glitz company and ask them, no, demand that they pay you for the past order of dresses. Even if they were late, they still have to pay us. You have to get the money.

(The radio is still on.)

ESTELA. I don't want to be too pushy. They're the only company that has been willing to give us a contract.

CARMEN. Then do it for Pancha and Rosalí. You haven't paid them and las pobrecitas can't even buy groceries.

ROSALI *(lying)*. I'm all right, don't worry about me.

ANA. Well, I'm not. Estela, just call.

(ESTELA thinks about it, then she decides to do it.)

ESTELA. Here I go.

(ANA turns off the radio. ESTELA picks up her cellphone, makes the call and waits.)

PANCHA. ¿Saben qué? My neighbor who works at the Del Monte canning factory is missing. I have a feeling they deported her. I'm so scared that I'll be waiting for the bus one day and they'll take me.

CARMEN. But you're legal.

PANCHA *(realizing)*. Ayy, I keep forgetting.

ESTELA. Hello … Can I speak to Mrs. Glitz? … Hello, this is Estela. Estela Garcia … No, but we're almost finished … I know we agreed that you would pay me for the last two weeks this Friday, but I was wondering, maybe, if it isn't too much trouble, if I could get an advance check … today … I know … I know … You're right, Mrs. Glitz … Ah … But my workers … I know, but I've got a lawyer working on that … I'll get it to you by next week … No, I mean it this time. Next week … OK, Mrs. Glitz … I'm sorry … Yes, I'll see you on Friday.

(ESTELA hangs up. Her face expresses worry and fear.)

CARMEN. ¿Qué te dijo la vieja?

PANCHA. What did she tell you?

ESTELA. She asked about my proof of employment papers again. Then she warned me that if la migra shuts us down, she won't pay us for all the work we've done.

CARMEN. ¡Mendiga vieja!

ANA. Do you think she would really do that?

(CARMEN and ESTELA talk among themselves.)

ESTELA. Amá, why is this happening to me? I'm going to get deported, aren't I, Amá?

CARMEN. Mira, supposing you do get deported, we'll get a coyote to smuggle you back in. Somehow we'll find the money.

ESTELA. But I would have let you and everybody down. I'll lose everything that I've worked for, the factory, and my self-respect. And I don't know if I can start again.

CARMEN. Estela, your Apá was thrown back to Mexico four times, but he kept coming back. If you did it once, you can do it again.

ESTELA. I hope so. *(Pulls herself together and continues working. She picks up a bundle of sewn skirts and looks at them. She discovers that they have been sewn wrong.)* Pancha, do you realize you sewed all of the size 4 skirts backwards?

PANCHA. I did? No, I didn't!

ESTELA. Look! This is the outside of the material and this is the inside. Have you been doing all the lots this way?

PANCHA. I think so.

ESTELA. ¡Ay, no! More repairs! Pancha, please do them again.

PANCHA. No! It's so hot. I don't even feel like working. How do you expect us to work with this heat?

ESTELA. Pancha, I'll help you take them apart.

ANA. Couldn't you open the door?

ESTELA. No!

PANCHA. I can't work like this.

ESTELA. We're going to have to. *(PANCHA grabs the skirt and begins to take them apart. ESTELA is looking at another lot and discovers the stained dresses that CARMEN hid.)* ¡Amá! What did I tell you about the mole?! *(ESTELA shoves a dress in CARMEN's face.)*

CARMEN. The stains are not so obvious. I was going to clean them, I swear. I didn't want you to see them and get worried.

ESTELA. It's going to be hell trying to take the stains out! *(ESTELA catches ANA accidentally burning the tulle.)* Not so close! You're burning the tulle! Pay close attention to your work or don't do it. Have you been burning it on the other dresses too?! *(ESTELA quickly looks at the dresses on the racks and those that ANA has finished ironing.)*

ANA. I thought if I did it this way it would be OK and save us time. I can't stand the heat and the steam.

ESTELA. Can't any of you do anything right? Do I have to do everything myself so that these dresses get finished? *(PANCHA gets busy pulling on the two pieces of material on the skirt instead of cutting the sewn thread one stitch at a time.)* Pancha, don't pull on them or you'll tear them. I said I was going to help you do the repairs.

PANCHA. I want to get out of here and go home.

ESTELA. You have to finish this work.

PANCHA. Not in this heat!

ANA. Estela, please open the door!

ESTELA. For the last time, I won't!

PANCHA. Then I'll open it. *(PANCHA walks determinedly towards the door. ESTELA stands in her way.)* We're all burning in here. I'm getting dizzy.

ESTELA. I'm sorry it's so hot, but the van may be out there and I don't want them to see anything.

PANCHA. It's so selfish of you to keep the door closed when we are all burning!

ESTELA. I'm burning too!

PANCHA. But you're the one with the criminal record! It's not fair that we are all paying for your fault. We are all legal now!

ESTELA. Then go! Open the door, then leave.

PANCHA. All right! I'll leave, but with my work. *(PANCHA grabs the skirts, begins pulling on them, tearing the material.)* Let's see what else I've done.

(PANCHA continues tearing. ESTELA tries to stop her by holding PANCHA's hands. PANCHA and ESTELA begin to get physical, almost ready to strike each other. ROSALI quickly steps between them to prevent them from hitting each other.)

CARMEN. Estela, ¡párale!

ROSALI. ¡Basta! ¡No se peleén!

(ROSALI faints and falls to the floor. ESTELA and PANCHA stop fighting.)

CARMEN. Rosalí!

ANA. Rosalí, are you all right?

CARMEN. What could be wrong with her?

PANCHA. It's this pinche heat! It's your fault, Estela. Here you have us all locked up! See what happened?!

ESTELA *(shakes ROSALI, who does not respond)*. Rosalí, please wake up!

PANCHA. Let's take her to the hospital!

CARMEN. ¡¿Pero que locura?! The hospital is three blocks away. We can't carry her, la migra is going to see us.

PANCHA. Ayy si, ¿entonces qué quiere? You want her to die?

CARMEN. She's not going to die!

PANCHA. And how do you know?

CARMEN. Don't exaggerate!

(While PANCHA and CARMEN argue, ANA thinks quickly of what to do. She searches around the bathroom for something. She finds ESTELA's perfume and grabs some tissue. ANA uses it to wake up ROSALI. ROSALI becomes conscious and PANCHA and CARMEN finally stop arguing.)

ROSALI. Ah…

PANCHA. Rosalí, you want to go to the hospital?

ROSALI. ¿Qué páso?

CARMEN. M'ija, you fainted.

ANA. Are you OK?

ROSALI. Sí … Sí … I'm OK.

PANCHA. I'm gonna take you home.

ROSALI. I'll just rest a little … I'll feel better …

PANCHA. You can't continue working like this. I'll take you home. It's no bother, because I'm going home myself.

(CARMEN gets a glass of water and an aspirin.)

CARMEN. Pobrecita, here, drink this.

ESTELA. Rosalí, I'm sorry.

PANCHA *(helps ROSALI up)*. Where's your bag? *(ROSALI points to it. PANCHA gets the bag.)* Let's go.

(PANCHA leaves with ROSALI without hesitation or saying goodbye. ESTELA fights the urge to cry.)

ESTELA *(to herself)*. I'm sorry, Rosalí.

CARMEN. Don't blame yourself. Something like this was going to happen.

ANA. Isn't Rosalí the only one who knows how to set up the over-lock machine?

(ANA and CARMEN look at each other worried. ESTELA has an expression of hopelessness. Lights slowly fade out.)

END OF ACT I

ACT II

SCENE 1

(Wednesday, August 9th, about 8:15 a.m. CARMEN and ESTELA are the only ones present, working silently. On the clock it is 8:15 a.m. On the calendar it is Wednesday, August 9.)

CARMEN. I don't think Pancha's coming back.

ESTELA. She's only an hour late. Maybe she went to visit Rosalí at her house.

CARMEN. Pancha is never late.

(Footsteps are heard outside. Then the code knock is heard. ESTELA smiles and goes to open the doors.)

ESTELA. See, Amá! I knew she would come. *(ESTELA rushes to open the door. ANA is at the door.)* Oh, it's just you.

(ANA quickly comes in carrying a brown paper bag with detergent, which she puts on the table.)

ANA. ¡Miren! Come look out the window. There's this strange homeless person outside. *(They go look.)*

CARMEN. What's so strange about him?

ANA. I don't recognize him.

ESTELA. So?

ANA. I think he's just disguised. He doesn't look desperate enough.

CARMEN. I've never seen him before.

ANA. I think he's a spy!

54

ESTELA. A spy?

ANA. Look! There's Pancha!

ESTELA. God! Thank you! She's come back!

CARMEN. But look, he's talking to her and she's pointing this way! *(They drop to the floor. A few seconds later they go back to looking.)* I wonder what he's asking her?

ESTELA. I wonder what she's telling him?

ANA. ¡Aguas! Here she comes.

(They scatter. ANA takes out the stain remover from the bag. CARMEN goes back to sewing. The code knock is heard and ESTELA opens the door. PANCHA comes in.)

ESTELA. Pancha, what did the bum ask you?

PANCHA. The bum? Ooo. He asked me where your Tormento lives.

ANA. I guess he wasn't a spy after all.

PANCHA. ¡N'ombre! He's just another one of his vago friends.

CARMEN. ¡Bola de viejos cochinos! No good drug addicts!

ESTELA. Ya! Stop talking about him!

CARMEN. Are you defending him? After what he did?

ANA *(aside)*. Amá, Estela finally told you?

CARMEN *(aside)*. No. I'm trying to get it out of her.

ESTELA. Forget it! I'll never tell you what happened on the date.

ANA. OK, Estela. Be like that. I'll never tell you anything either.

(ESTELA doesn't budge. ANA and CARMEN give up.)

CARMEN. Panchita, we were afraid you wouldn't come back.

PANCHA. Why?

CARMEN. Well, after what happened yesterday.

PANCHA. I have to come to work even if I don't want to … I went to visit Rosalí this morning.

ANA. How is she doing?

PANCHA. She's doing better.

ESTELA. Is there any chance of her coming back this week?

PANCHA. No se. She looks pale. This heat will be bad for her. I'm surprised I didn't faint myself.

ESTELA. Maybe I will get a fan.

PANCHA. Estela, what do you want me to work on?

ESTELA. I don't know how we are going to manage without her. Pancha, please finish the zippers that Rosalí was working on.

CARMEN. Estela, give me the manual for the over-lock machine. I'm going to try and set it up myself.

ESTELA. Alli esta en el cajon. We'll just have to go on without her. Ana, did you get the stain remover?

ANA. It's on the table. How many dresses need washing?

ESTELA. Twelve. I should put my mother to wash them, but since she'll be busy with the over-lock I guess I'll do them.

ANA. How many dresses have we finished?

ESTELA. They're on the racks. And there are a couple in that box that just need ironing.

ANA (looking at the racks). That's all?

ESTELA. I found ten dresses with the tulle burnt in them. Those were almost finished, but now the tulle has to be replaced.

ANA. I guess I'll do that.

ESTELA. Amá, can you stay late today?

CARMEN. Pues sí.

ESTELA. Ana, will you stay late too?

ANA. Stay late? … Sure.

(ANA irons a dress carefully and slowly. ESTELA observes ANA for a few seconds.)

ESTELA. Ana, can you iron faster? Just make them look decent.

(ANA frowns at her suggestion and looks to PANCHA, who is attaching hanging strings on the dresses next to her.)

ANA *(to PANCHA)*. It's not that I don't iron fast enough, it's that whenever I finish ironing a dress I stop for a minute to really look at it. I never realized just how much work, puro lomo, as my mother would say, went into making it. Then I imagine the dress at Bloomingdale's and I see a tall and skinny woman looking at it. She instantly gets it and with no second thoughts she says "charge it!" She doesn't think of the life of the dress before the rack, of the labor put into it. I shake the dress a little and try to forget it's not for me. I place a plastic bag over it then I put it on the rack and push it away. It happens to me with every dress.

PANCHA. What an imagination. So what are you gonna study when you go to college next year? Where are you going?

ANA. To New York University. I'm going to study writing.

CARMEN. Así es que you better be quiet, don't tell her any chisme or one day you're gonna read about it.

PANCHA. And you think you'll make it?

ANA. I think so.

PANCHA. Pos, I do think you're a bit loquita, but if that's what you need. I think you'll make it.

ANA. Gracias, Pancha.

(PANCHA smiles at ANA, seeing her differently for the first time. Meanwhile, CARMEN is frustrated with the over-lock machine.)

CARMEN. ¡Ayy no! ¡No puedo! I try and I try and I can't! ¡Esta cochinada no sirve!

ESTELA. But what can we do? Who else could do it? Can you do it, Pancha?

PANCHA. I don't know anything about those new machines.

ESTELA. Amá, give me the manual. *(ESTELA grabs the manual and begins to work on the machine. Talking to the machine:)* Please, maquinita. If you behave I'll put on you all the oil you want. Maquinita, if you love me, help me.

CARMEN *(touching her stomach)*. Ana, come here, quick. Feel my stomach. *(ANA puts her hand over CARMEN's stomach.)* Can you feel the baby kicking?

ANA. No … Amá, are you sure you're pregnant?

CARMEN. I think so. Aver, Pancha, tell me if you feel anything.

PANCHA. I'm busy, Doña Carmen.

CARMEN. Just come quick, Panchita. Ana doesn't believe me.

(PANCHA gets up from her chair and goes over to CARMEN. She places her hand on CARMEN's stomach.)

PANCHA. I don't feel anything. I think the heat is getting to you too.

CARMEN. ¿Cómo puede ser? I can feel it!

(PANCHA nods her head and walks away fanning herself. She heads to the bathroom.)

ANA. How many months should you be pregnant by now? I haven't noticed you getting any bigger.

CARMEN. I don't know. I've always been fat. I haven't noticed either.

ANA. Have you the symptoms?

CARMEN. Not all of them, but I've been pregnant enough times to know.

ANA. Are you going to keep it?

CARMEN. What do you mean?

ANA. You don't have to have it.

CARMEN. Ana, I don't want to talk about this.

(Spotlight on PANCHA. PANCHA stands on the toilet in front of the small window. She opens the window and bathes her face with the breeze. PANCHA begins to cry.)

PANCHA. Que bonito viento. Wind, that's what I am. *(Touching her stomach.)* Empty, like an old rag … *(Praying.)* Diosito, why don't you make me a real woman? If I can't have children, why did you make me a woman? *(PANCHA wipes her tears.)*

(Lights come on.)

ESTELA *(talking to the machine)*. Maquinita, I'm going to set you up even if it's the last thing I do in this country. *(She holds the manual and follows directions.)* All right. Five threads. They all start from their spools onto the holes, then straight down, into the loops. Then they turn, go in between more loops underneath, then they all go into their needles. Then the electricity comes on … *(She turns on the machine.)* … I insert a piece of material, step on the pedal and … Ta-da! A chain of interwoven threads! I did it!

CARMEN. You fixed it? ¿Pero cómo?

ESTELA. I persisted and I did it!

CARMEN. ¡Mira que inteligente!

ANA. That's great, Estela! Now we don't have to worry about it anymore. *(They hear footsteps outside. They instantly freeze and become silent. They look to each other then CARMEN, ANA and PANCHA quickly go to their purses. Someone is heard outside, then letters are slipped in through the mail slot. The WOMEN relax.)* Just the mailman …

(The WOMEN suddenly realize that it probably means bad news for ESTELA. ESTELA picks up an envelope and reads it. No one asks what it says out of respect for her, but they all know it's another letter from the lawyer. ESTELA opens it and is about to read it when they hear footsteps outside. They grab their "Green Cards"—Permanent Residency cards from their purses. ESTELA hides behind CARMEN. Then the code knock is heard. The WOMEN rush to the door. ESTELA opens the door and ROSALI is behind the bar door.)

EVERYONE. What are you doing here?!

ESTELA. Aren't you suppose to be resting?

ROSALI. I was in bed and I kept imagining Estela getting deported. So I had to come back. I know how badly you must need the over-lock machine.

ESTELA. I fixed it!

ROSALI *(disappointed)*. You did? Well, where are the zippers so I can get started now?

PANCHA. I finished all the zippers.

ROSALI. You did?

ESTELA. Rosalí, I'd rather you go back and get well.

ROSALI. No, Estela, I'm fine. I can help.

ESTELA. It's not worth it if we're fighting and getting sick because of this heat.

ROSALI. It wasn't just the heat … I hadn't eaten and that's why I fainted. I didn't want you to think it was your fault.

PANCHA. But why do you need to lose weight? 'Tas flaca. *(ROSALI smiles, but doesn't believe PANCHA.)*

CARMEN. Did you eat already, you still look pale?

ROSALI. No, I'm not hungry, Doña Carmen.

CARMEN. But that's what you have been saying and look what happened. Come on, eat something.

ROSALI. I am not hungry.

ANA. Rosalí, you can't see yourself the way we see you and that's why you think you're fat.

CARMEN. Rosalí, you need to eat something.

ROSALI. I'm not hungry!

CARMEN. You need to eat something!

(ROSALI looks at each of them and finally reveals the truth.)

ROSALI. I'm not hungry because I've been living on diet pills.

CARMEN. So that's the secret diet? Ayy, Rosalí, don't you know those cochinadas are no good?

ANA. They're real bad for you because I read they're addictive.

ROSALI. I know. When I fainted I saw my body lying there, I thought I was going to die. I couldn't feel my body. And I just kept seeing Estela being deported. Estela, I want to come back to work. This is more important to me than being a size two.

ESTELA *(embraces ROSALI).* Gracias… *(Beat)* Can you work late?

ROSALI. Claro.

ESTELA. And you too, Pancha?

PANCHA. Pos bueno.

CARMEN. Entonces todas a trabajar!

(The WOMEN go to their sewing stations. ESTELA takes out her notebook and dictates the work.)

ESTELA. Amá, let Rosalí do the over-lock work, she's faster. I want you to do lots size zero through six. Pancha, you do lots size 6 through 12. Ana, you know what to do.

(ESTELA takes control and the WOMEN are determined to finish. The machines roar like race cars taking off. Lights slowly fade.)

SCENE 2

(Thursday, August 10th, about 2:00 a.m. Lights come on. It is 2:00 a.m., and street sounds are heard outside. ROSALI looks around and then stares at her stomach.)

ROSALI. Did you hear that?

ANA. No, what?

ROSALI. A stomach growling. Whose stomach was it?

ESTELA. I don't know, but I'm hungry.

ANA. Me too. Amá, is there any rice left?

ROSALI. Did you hear it again?

PANCHA. Rosalí, it's your panza.

ROSALI. Yeah, it's me! I haven't heard my stomach growling in so long.

ESTELA. What's there to eat?

CARMEN. I might have something in my purse. Why don't we make something?

PANCHA. All this noise is driving me crazy. I'm going deaf.

(PANCHA turns on the radio. CARMEN gets up, looks around the table then in the refrigerator. All the WOMEN search in their purses for food.)

CARMEN. Aaaa, I found something. Tortillas and … the mole!

ALL. Not the mole!

PANCHA. I've got something. *(PANCHA takes out a large amount of food from her purse. The WOMEN are surprised with every item she takes out: a box of fried chicken, a hamburger, a bag of chips, a bag of cookies and a Diet Coke.)* I'm on a diet!

CARMEN *(aside)*. Se ve.

(On the radio a "cumbia" has just finished. Then a DISC JOCKEY with a very mellow voice comes on the air.)

DISC JOCKEY *(V.O.)*. It's 2:25 a.m. on an early Thursday morning … I'm falling asleep here to pay my bills. And if you're listening now, you probably are too. So this is for you night owls! The ones that do the night shifts no one wants to do!

(The song "Tequila" blasts on the radio. The WOMEN are so sleepy, they jump around to the music trying to awaken. They eat and shake at the same time. Lights slowly fade.)

SCENE 3

(Same day, about 2:00 p.m. Lights come on. It is Thursday, August 10. On the clock it is 2 p.m. The WOMEN are wearing the same clothes as the day before. As usual, it is extremely hot.)

CARMEN *(smelling her armpits)*. Phueeehh! ¡Fuchi! I stink. Aquí huele a pura cuchupeta y pedo. Phuehhh! Who farted?

ESTELA. Amá, it's probably you who did it. Like they say, the one who smells it first is the one who has it underneath her skirt.

ANA. ¡Que calor! It feels like we're in hell!

PANCHA. How many more dresses to finish, Estela?

ESTELA. Fifteen.

ROSALI. Only fifteen?!

CARMEN. Dios mio, ya mero acabamos.

ESTELA *(counting dresses on rack)*. 184, 185, 186. No, we only need 14!

ANA. What a relief! We're almost finished.

(ANA decides to take off her blouse, leaving on her sweaty bra.)

CARMEN *(shocked at ANA's actions)*. Ana, what are you doing?!

ANA. All this steam has me sweating like a pig.

CARMEN. We're sweating too, but we don't go taking our clothes off.

ANA. So why don't you? We're all women. We all have the same.

CARMEN. Not really. You have bigger chichis.

ANA. And you have a bigger panza!

CARMEN. That's because I'm pregnant!

ESTELA. You mean we're definitely going to have another baby brat to take care of?

ANA. Amá, do you really want to have it?

PANCHA. Doña Carmen, give it to me if you don't want it.

CARMEN. I can't just get rid of it, either way … But I don't want to have it.

PANCHA. But you're lucky, Doña Carmen.

CARMEN. No. It seems all I do is have children. One after another. I'm tired of this! I can't have this baby. I'll die. Last time I was pregnant the doctor said I almost didn't make it.

ANA. Amá, I didn't know that happened.

CARMEN. Every time your Apá touches me, the next day I'm pregnant. When he would leave me in Mexico to go to el norte, he would leave me pregnant so no man would look at me and desire me. I was very beautiful.

ANA. You still are, Amá.

CARMEN. I was always scared of him. And I let myself get fat after you were born hoping he would be disgusted by me and not touch me anymore.

ANA. Why didn't you just say "No"?

CARMEN. Because, M'ija, I was never taught how to say no.

PANCHA *(comes forward and confesses)*. It's easy, Doña Carmen. You tell him "No!" and you get out from the bed.

ANA *(realizing what PANCHA is saying)*. Pancha?

PANCHA. And then you take the blanket.

(ANA embraces PANCHA as the WOMEN laugh.)

ANA *(to the WOMEN)*. Aren't you hot in those clothes? I feel sticky. I'm going to take off my pants.

(ANA takes off her pants. She is left wearing her bra and panties.)

CARMEN. Ana, aren't you embarrassed?

ANA. Why? You already think I'm fat.

CARMEN. You know, Ana, you're not bad looking. If you lost 20 pounds you would be very beautiful.

ANA. Story of my life … Go ahead. Pick on me.

CARMEN. Why don't you lose weight? Last time you lost weight you were so thin and beatifuller.

ANA. I like myself. Why should I?

PANCHA. Doña Carmen, Ana is very pretty. She looks good the way she is.

ANA. Thank you, Pancha.

CARMEN. It's because she's young. At this age young girls should try to make themselves as attractive as possible.

ANA. Why? Why not always? You're overweight too.

CARMEN. But I'm already married.

ANA. Is that it? Make myself attractive so that I can catch a man?

ESTELA *(sarcastically)*. Ana, listen to them, learn now, "or you'll end up like Estela."

ANA. Amá, I do want to lose weight. But part of me doesn't because my weight says to everyone, "Fuck you!"

CARMEN. ¡Ave Maria Purissima!

ANA. It says, "How dare you try to define me and tell me what I have to be and look like!" So I keep it on. I don't want to be a sex object.

ESTELA. Me neither!

CARMEN. ¡Otra!

ROSALI. What's wrong with being a sex object? What's wrong with wanting to be thin and sexy?

ESTELA. Because I want to be taken seriously, to be considered a person ... You know with Andrés, on our date ...

CARMEN. ¡Aver cuentanos! What happened on that infamous date?

ESTELA. On our date I got all fixed up ... Then he showed up with jeans and a t-shirt and he smelled like he had been drinking ... He told me he wanted to take me to a... motel. He said because there he could kiss me and give me what I wanted ... He said, "I don't care if you're fat. I like you even better; more to grab." That got me so angry! I thought he was interested in me because he was impressed that I owned this factory, my "intelligence," that I ... "I'm smart" ... When am I going to meet that man who will see the real me?

CARMEN. So that's what happened.

ROSALI. Pues if he has a brother, tell him about me. I think I'm going to die a virgin.

ANA. You're still a virgin?! Dang!

PANCHA. ¿Pero tu Johnny? Nothing?

ROSALI. Nothing. I've felt fat ever since I can remember and I didn't want anybody to touch me until I got thin.

ANA. Is that why you were starving yourself?

ROSALI. That's part of it.

ESTELA. Rosalí, you're not fat.

ROSALI. Of course I am. Look at my nalgas ... And my hips! Paresen de elefante.

ANA. No they don't!

ROSALI. I look like a cow.

CARMEN. You look like a cow? Where does that leave us?

PANCHA. Rosalí, you're so skinny in comparison to all of us.

ROSALI. No I'm not. Here, look at my fat hips.

(ROSALI pulls down her pants and shows them her hips.)

ESTELA. That's nothing. ¡Mira!

(ESTELA pulls down her pants and shows ROSALI her hips.)

CARMEN *(to ROSALI)*. At least you have a waist!

(CARMEN pulls down her skirt and shows ROSALI her stomach.)

PANCHA. ¡Uuuu! That's nothing, Doña Carmen!

(PANCHA raises her skirt and shows them her stomach.)

ROSALI. But you don't understand. I've got all these stretch marks on my arms…

(ROSALI opens her blouse and shows them the stretch marks close to her breasts.)

ESTELA. They're small. I have stretch marks that run from my hips to my ankles.

(ESTELA takes off her pants to show them.)

CARMEN. Stretch marks?! Stretch marks!! You want to see stretch marks? *(CARMEN lifts her blouse and exposes her stretch marks and scars.)* Stretch marks!!!

(ANA sits back as she watches the WOMEN slowly undressing. They continue to compare body parts ad-libbing. Finally they are all in their underwear and they stop to notice CARMEN's stretch marks.)

ANA. Amá, what's that scar you have on your stomach?

CARMEN. This one? That was Estela.

ANA. It's such a big scar.

CARMEN. Estela was a big baby.

ESTELA. I gave you the most trouble, didn't I?

CARMEN. A-ha. But that's OK. I've heard Elizabeth Potaylor had one just like it.

PANCHA *(suddenly realizing)*. Look how we are? What if somebody came in and saw us like this?

CARMEN *(fanning her breasts)*. Pero que bien se siente. It feels so good to be rid of these clothes and let it all hang out.

ANA. Pues sí. Nobody is watching us. Who cares how we look.

ESTELA. So this is how we look without clothes?

CARMEN. Just as fat and beautiful ...

(They all hug in a semi-circle laughing triumphantly.)

ANA. We can finally relax.

ESTELA. We're not finished yet.

ROSALI. Estela, all we need are 14 dresses.

PANCHA. Those we can finish tomorrow for sure.

CARMEN. So what are we going to do to celebrate?

ESTELA. To celebrate what? Finishing on time for the first time?

PANCHA. No. All of us, most of us, finally being legal.

CARMEN. It's true. And once you get you "greencard" you can do anything you want. Tengo fe … Estela, I've been thinking … You know what we could do? We could copy the patterns for these dresses, make the dresses ourselves, and have a fashion show. Maybe we could model them ourselves.

(The WOMEN laugh at the thought.)

ANA. No, that's a great idea! Why don't we make them in larger sizes too?

PANCHA. Está loquita, but sometimes she makes sense. We could probably sell more if we made them in larger sizes.

ROSALI. You know what we could also do? Jaime could sell them in the swap meet. If they sell, little by little we could grow …

ESTELA *(jumping in)*. And from there, if we make a lot of money, more money than what we're making now, maybe we can rent a place downtown on Broadway and start a boutique!!

ANA. But we'll need a name.

ROSALI. Well, why not just Estela Garcia?

ANA. I was thinking of something more French.

CARMEN. No. A French name would make it sound chafas. No, Estela Garcia sounds fine.

PANCHA. Estela, maybe you could go to school and study fashion design and design our dresses.

ESTELA. Yeah. I could do that.

(They all stop to imagine the possibilities.)

CARMEN. So what are we doing to celebrate?

ESTELA. First let's finish, then we can talk about celebrating.

(They go back to work. CARMEN takes off her glasses as she fans her face.)

CARMEN. Que calor. I'll be glad when all of this is over.

ANA. Estela, can we please open the door?

PANCHA. Open the door? ¿Pa qué? So people that pass by can see us like this?

ROSALI. But it's so hot!

ANA. I don't think they're coming. Besides we're almost finished.

(The WOMEN look to ESTELA for a decision.)

ESTELA. OK … Amá, open the door.

(CARMEN goes to open the door. She turns back to ESTELA as if to make sure. CARMEN opens the door and fans herself with it. Beat. CARMEN holds the door wide open and walks outside. The WOMEN can't believe their eyes. A few seconds later CARMEN runs back in screaming.)

CARMEN. Estela! It's out there! ¡La Migra! I.C.E.! They're coming!!

(CARMEN shuts the door. All the WOMEN immediately get dressed.)

ESTELA. No! It's not fair! We were almost finished!!

(The WOMEN dig into their purses for their cards. ESTELA can only cry in desperation. She cannot find her clothes and has to head for the door in her slip. ROSALI and ANA peek through the curtains and quickly make a realization.)

ROSALI. Doña Carmen, that's not I.C.E.!

ANA. It's the police!

CARMEN. The police? *(She peeks through the curtain.)* ¡¿Cómo?!

ANA. That's the guy I thought was a spy. He's an undercover cop!

ROSALI. Like in the movies.

ANA. It's a drug bust!

ESTELA. Where?

ROSALI. I think it's el Tormento's house.

(ESTELA moves for the door.)

ANA. ¡Sí, el Tormento! They're taking him away.

(ESTELA and ANA jump up in excitement.)

CARMEN. That's what he deserves!

(The police are heard driving away.)

PANCHA. That's good they're taking him away in the van. ¡Bola de viejos cochinos!

(The WOMEN laugh together. Then ANA stops laughing.)

ANA. Amá, was that the same van you saw Monday?

CARMEN *(nodding her head hesitantly)*. I think so.

ANA. On Tuesday?

CARMEN. I think so.

ANA. On Wednesday?

CARMEN *(sheepishly)*. Pos sí. *(She puts on her glasses.)*

ANA. Amá, that wasn't la migra. Everyone knows the I.C.E. vans have a seal that says immigration on it not D.E.A.!

CARMEN. I didn't.

ESTELA. How could you not know?

CARMEN. Pos no se; all those years of being undocumented I always imagined they were black.

PANCHA & ROSALI. Ayy, Doña Carmen!!!

CARMEN. Phueehhh! Tanto pedo y para nada.

ESTELA. Thank God! ¡Que susto!

CARMEN. It's time to retire!

(They laugh in relief then they become silent.)

ANA. Well, it's over … for now. *(Beat.)*

ESTELA. If you want to take the rest of the day off … We'll finish tomorrow.

PANCHA. We can go?

ESTELA. Yes. I know how tired you must be. Go ahead. I'll stay and continue working.

ROSALI. I can't wait to go home and take a shower.

CARMEN. Si, porfavor, bañate … Tomorrow, I'm going to make a fresh batch of mole.

PANCHA *(scared for her life)*. Doña Carmen, why don't you make some rice?

(ANA, PANCHA and ROSALI immediately run out.)

CARMEN *(muttering to them)*. Ingratas! *(To ESTELA.)* Are you sure you won't need us anymore?

ESTELA. No. Now go! Before I change my mind. Don't you want to go outside?

(They gather their bags and quickly leave. ESTELA is left alone. Lights fade a little. She turns on the radio to a mellow

jazz station. She goes around doing a final clean up, turning off lights and machines. She stops, recalling the five of them in their underwear, fantasizing about their own boutique. She grins to herself. She whispers.)

ESTELA *(cont'd).* Large sizes?

(ESTELA shakes her head, dismissing the idea, but then stops and runs to a pile of stocked material. She eagerly searches and finds a roll of red fabric. ESTELA excitedly runs to a station and begins taking her measurements. As the lights slowly fade, we see ESTELA measuring herself with pride and pleasure, half laughing to herself, half defiantly … about to design and make her first dress. Lights slowly fade to black.)

SCENE 4

(Friday, August 11th, about 2:25 p.m. Lights come on. There are no more dresses on the racks. It is Friday, on the clock it is 2:25 p.m. ANA and PANCHA are busy blowing up balloons. ROSALI is cleaning up. There is a birthday cake with a large candle of the number "35." A large sign reads: "Happy Birthday Estela." Footsteps are heard outside. ANA runs to turn off the electricity, the WOMEN hide … The door opens.)

WOMEN. Surprise!!!!!

(ROSALI takes a picture. CARMEN stands motionless holding a pot.)

ANA. Amá, we thought you were …
ROSALI. Doña Carmen, what's wrong?

CARMEN. I just got back from the doctor.

PANCHA. What did she tell you?

ANA. ¿Amá?

CARMEN. She says I'm not pregnant.

ANA. Then why are you sad?

CARMEN. She says, "it's only menopause." When you reach menopause it's over. You're no longer a woman. Se te seca allí abajo.

ANA. Amá, you are a real woman.

CARMEN. What I should be is a grandmother by now, but the way you and Estela are going you'll never get married and I'll have to support you … ¿Y Estela?

ROSALI. She hasn't returned from delivering the dresses. She should be coming soon.

CARMEN. Here. *(Gives ROSALI the pot.)* I made rice.

(They hear footsteps outside. ANA turns off the lights. The door opens.)

WOMEN. Surprise!!!

(ROSALI takes another picture. Lights come on. ESTELA stands shocked in her new dress.)

ESTELA. You remembered?

ROSALI *(gives ESTELA a gift)*. Happy thirty-fifth birthday, you old maid!

CARMEN *(referring to her dress)*. Estela, did you make it? Que bonita te ves, very nice. You see you're not ugly, you just didn't know how to dress.

ESTELA *(hugs ROSALI)*. I brought a gift for all of you.

(ESTELA goes outside and brings in a large fan.)

PANCHA. Now the boss treats us pretty good.

ESTELA. Because now I have money.

CARMEN. Did Mrs. Glitz finally pay you?

ESTELA. Yes, she paid me, but she kept threatening me … I've written out all the checks.

(ESTELA pulls out the checks from her bag. She distributes them, the first check going to PANCHA.)

PANCHA *(looking at her check)*. This is the biggest check I've ever gotten in my life.

(ESTELA gives ROSALI her check.)

ROSALI. Too bad I've already spent it on the Americana Express.

CARMEN. ¡Válgame! I didn't realize how much money you owed me.

ANA *(looks at her check, disappointed)*. Estela, come here. *(ANA and ESTELA talk among themselves.)* Estela, how come I only get this much?

ESTELA. I took out for taxes.

ANA. Taxes? But you're not reporting …

CARMEN. How much do you have left?

ESTELA. About two thousand dollars. I'll send the lawyer some more money today. Maybe they won't take me to court.

PANCHA. But if they deport you and take everything, we won't be able to work towards the boutique.

ROSALI. We're also going to have to look for another job.

(The WOMEN stare at the floor.)

ANA. Back to McDonald's. *(Beat.)*

PANCHA. Estela, I know my husband isn't going to like it, but here. *(PANCHA extends her check to ESTELA.)* Take it. Pay me back when you can.

ESTELA. Pancha, are you sure?

PANCHA. No, pero, take it before I change my mind.

ESTELA. Muchas gracias … *(They try hugging, but they find it difficult, it's awkward. To herself).* Let's see. How much more do I need? *(CARMEN stares at her check for a few more seconds and slowly says goodbye to it.)*

CARMEN. Ten, ten. Take mine too. What kind of mother would I be if I didn't give it back?

ESTELA *(hugs CARMEN).* ¡Que buena es!

CARMEN. You see, ¿No que no te quiero? It's because I love you that I make your life so miserable.

ESTELA. Don't love me so much. *(ROSALI thinks about it too.)*

ROSALI. I guess the Americana Express can wait … Here is my check too.

(ESTELA hugs ROSALI. Now they all look to ANA. ANA holds her check tightly.)

ANA. No, not me … I'm going to buy a PC … I can't. *(The WOMEN don't say anything, but continue staring at ANA.)* I really need this PC. I have this essay I have to type up for a contest … All right … Take half of it.

(ESTELA semi-hugs ANA.)

ESTELA. Excuse me for just a minute. I have to make a phone call. *(ESTELA picks up her cell phone and makes a call.)* Hello … May I speak to Mrs. Glitz? This is Estela Garcia.

I'm just calling to thank you for keeping your word and finally paying us today. I also wanted to tell you that you are a mean, wicked, bitter, unsympathetic, greedy, rude, awful …

ANA. Capitalist!

ESTELA. Capitalist! … No! We quit … Yeah, well I'll see you in hell.

(The WOMEN are shocked, incredulous of her actions.)

CARMEN. ¡Maldita! What have you done?

PANCHA. You got us fired, didn't you?

ESTELA. No, we quit. *(ESTELA laughs excitedly.)* … Don't worry about the work. I got us a contract with Señor Vasquez!

EVERYONE. Señor Vasquez!!!

CARMEN. How did you convince him?

ESTELA. I just told him that we are the most hardworking women he could ever ask for. I know, I lied, but I got it.

EVERYONE. ¡Ayy!

(All the WOMEN embrace excitedly. ROSALI brings out the birthday cake. They sing "Happy Birthday" not realizing that ROSALI is holding the cake backwards and it reads 53 instead of 35. They stop halfway through and turn it.)

ESTELA. Fifty three?! *(They continue singing.)*

ROSALI. Ana, light up the candle so I can take a picture … *(ANA lights up the candle.)* OK, Estela, blow out the candle.

(ESTELA stops to make a wish then blows it out. ROSALI takes a picture of her.)

ANA. What did you wish for?

ESTELA. Maybe when you get back from New York you'll see.

(ANA and PANCHA give their gift to ESTELA.)

ROSALI. Ana, here, take a picture of us to remember this week... *(ROSALI gives ANA the camera. The WOMEN gather for the photo.)* ANA. OK! Ready? ... One ... two ... three!

(The WOMEN suddenly hold up their "Green Cards"— Temporary Residence Cards.)

WOMEN. Green!!!

(The WOMEN freeze in a pool of light. ANA steps out and turns to the audience. The WOMEN exit backstage. Spotlight on ANA.)

ANA. I always took their work for granted, to be simple and unimportant. I was not proud to be working there at the beginning. I was only glad to know that because I was educated, I wasn't going to end up like them. I was going to be better than them. And I wanted to show them how much smarter and liberated I was. I was going to teach them about the women's liberation movement, about sexual liberation and all the things a so-called educated American woman knows. But in their subtle ways they taught me about resistance. About a battle no one was fighting for them except themselves. About the loneliness of being immigrant women in a country that looks down on us for being mothers and submissive women. With their work that seems simple and unimportant, they are fighting ... Perhaps the greatest thing I learned from them is that women are powerful, especially when working together … As for me, well, I settled for going the public library and using a public computer and I wrote an essay on my experience and I was awarded a fellowship. So I went to New York and was a starving writer for some time before I went to New York University. When I came back the plans for making the boutique were no longer a dream, but a reality. *(ANA picks up a beautiful designer jacket and puts it on.)* Because I now wear original designs from Estela Garcia's boutique, "Real Women Have Curves."

(The lights come on and all the WOMEN enter the door wearing new evening gowns and accessories designed by ESTELA. The WOMEN parade down the theater aisles voguing in a fashion-show style. They take their bows, continue voguing, and slowly exit. Lights slowly fade out.)

The End

GLOSSARY

A trabajar - To work it is

Abraza(r) - to hug

Abuelita - grandmother, granny

Adios - goodbye

Aguas - look out

Ahora si - OK, now you tell me!

Alli esta en el cajon - It's there in the drawer

Amá - mama

¡Andenle! - Come on!

Apá - papa

Aqui huele a pura cuchupeta y a pedo - It smells like pussy and fart

Así es que - therefore/so

Asi hazlo - Do it this way

¡Ave Maria Purissima! - Oh holy Mary of God!

Aver - Let's see, to have

Aver cuentanos - Come on tell us

¡Aver dime, condenada! - Damn

¡Ayy! - Ahh!, Oh!

¡Ayy que buenote! - He's so fine!

bañate - take a shower

Barrio - neighborhood

Basta - enough

Besa(r) - to kiss

Blusas - blouses

Bola de viejos cochinos - bunch of dirty old men

Bueno - well, good

Buenos dias - good morning

Callense - be quiet

Chafas - tacky

Chicharron - pork rinds

Chichis - boobs, titties
Chisme - to gossip
Chismosa - gossip monger
Claro - of course
Cochinadas - junk
Como es - see how you are
¿Cómo estas? - How are you?
¿Como puede ser? - How can it be?
Corazón - heart
Coyote - people across the border illegally for a price
Cumbia - Latin music from the Caribbean
¿de qué te apuras? - Why worry?
Desgraciada - ungrateful
Dios mio, ya mero acabamos - Oh, God, we're almost finished.
Diosito - God
Doña - a term of respect, literally meaning "old mother;" usually applied to the oldest woman present
¿Dónde los escondo? - Where shall I hide them?
¡Echame la culpa! - Blame me!
El Tormento - the heartthrob, or "crush," or tormentor
Enojona - grouch
Entonces a la fuerza - then by force
¿Entonces que quiere? - Then what do you want?
¡Entonces todas a trabajar! - Then to work it is!
¡Esa perra! - That bitch!
Eso - that
¡Esta cochinada no sirve! - This piece of junk doesn't work!
Está loquita - she's a little crazy
Estamos odidas - We are screwed
Fresas - strawberries, snooty upper class people in Mexico
Gringa - Anglo-Saxon woman
Hasta mañana - until tomorrow
Hijole - short for son of a bitch

¡Hora si que estamos bien jodidas! - Now we're really messed up!

Horita te lo coso - I'll sew it for you right now

Hoyc - listen

Huevona - lazy, good for nothing

La migra - US Immigration and Naturalization Service officials, border patrol

Las pobrecitas - the poor women

Listos para chupar - delicious enough to suck

Lonchera - the lunch mobile

Loquita - a little crazy

Maldita - goddamned woman

Maquinita - little sewing machine

¡Mendiga vieja! - Damn witch!

¡Mentirosa! - Liars!

Metiche - nosy

Mi viejo - my husband, my old man

M'ija - my daughter

Mira(r) - to look, Look!

Mira que inteligente - look how smart

Mira que paresco - see what I look like

¡Miren! - Look!

¡Miren cómo coquetea! - Look how she flirts!

Mole - a sauce made of chocolate and chili

Nada - nothing

Nalgas - buttocks

Ni lo mande dios - god forbid

No le da verguenza - she's not ashamed

No mas mira que paresco - Just look what I look like

No mas ven a ver - Just come take a look

¡No puedo! - I can't

No que no te quiero - And you say I don't love you

No se - I don't know

¡No se peleen! - don't fight
No seas mensa - don't be dumb
No seas terca - don't be stubborn
No te hagas de rogar - don't make us beg
No te va hacer daño - It won't do you any harm
N'ombre - no way
Nopal - cactus
¡Otra! - Another one!
¿Pa que? - For what?
Panza - stomach, belly
Panzonas - pregnant
Parele - stop it
Paresen de elefante - they look like they belong on an elephant
Patrona - boss
Pegame - hit me
Pero - but
¿Pero cómo? - But how?
Pero no puede ser - but it can't be
Pero que bien se siente - but it feels so good
Pero que loqura - what insanity
Pero tu - but you
Pinche - damn
¡Pinche rata! - Damn rat!
Pobre - poor
Pobre mujer - poor woman
Pobrecita - poor baby
Por favor - please
Por fin - finally
¿Pos cómo le hiciste? - Well, how did you do it?
Pos no nos queda otra - well we have no choice
Pos no se - Well, I don't know
¿Pos qué paso? - Well, what happened?
Pos yo ya no veo - I can't see a thing

Pues - Well
Pues por que no - well why not
Puro lomo - all back
Que bonita, te ves - How pretty you look
Que bonito - how pretty
Que bonito viento - what beautiful wind
¡Que buena es! - How good you are!
¡Que calor! - It's so hot!
¿Qué hiciste? - What did you do?
¿Que le pico? - What bit you?
Que locura - What madness
Que metiches - how nosey
¿Qué pasó? - What happened?
¡Que susto! - What scare!
¿Que te dijo la vieja? - What did the old hag tell you?
Rapido - quickly
¿Saben qué? - You know what?
"Se prohibe chismear!" - "Gossiping is Prohibited!"
Se te seca alli abajo - it gets dried down there
Se ve - It shows
Señor - mister, Mr., Sir
Si, ya se fue - Yes, he's already left.
Tambien - also
Tan pequeña - so young
Tanto pedo y para nada - all this fuss/worrying and for nothing
'Tas flaca - You're skinny
Ten - Take it
Tengo fe - I have faith
Tul - Tulle – "tul", a synthetic material used for petty coats
Vago - loser, lazy, good for nothing
Valgame - oh my
Vamonos - let's go

Vamos a estar como gallinas enjauladas - we're going to be
like caged chickens
Vas a verlo - you'll see
Venganse - Come you all
¿Verá que sí? - Isn't it true?
Y los … - And the …
¿Y por qué no me habias dicho? - Why hadn't you told me?
¿Y tu? - And you?
Ya basta - enough already
Ya llego mi viejo - my husband is here
¡Ya ni la friegas! - You blew it